ANCIENT MONUMENTS

in the care of the Ministry of Works

Illustrated Regional Guide No. 1

NORTHERN ENGLAND

by

THE RT. HON. LORD HARLECH

P.C., K.G., G.C.M.G., F.S.A.

Formerly First Commissioner of Works

LONDON

HER MAJESTY'S STATIONERY OFFICE

1951

First Edition 1935

Bound Edition 1951

Sixth Impression with amendments 1962

Crown Copyright Reserved

Published by
HER MAJESTY'S STATIONERY OFFICE

To be purchased from
York House, Kingsway, London w.c.2
423 Oxford Street, London w.1
13A Castle Street, Edinburgh 2
109 St. Mary Street, Cardiff
39 King Street, Manchester 2
50 Fairfax Street, Bristol 1
35 Smallbrook, Ringway, Birmingham 5
80 Chichester Street, Belfast 1
or through any bookseller

Price 4s. 6d. net

*Printed in England under the authority of
Her Majesty's Stationery Office
by Fosh & Cross Ltd., Wt.2584 K48*

CONTENTS

ILLUSTRATIONS

PREFACE TO THE FIRST EDITION

The purpose of these regional guides to the monuments in the ownership or guardianship of the Office of Works under the Ancient Monuments Acts of 1913 and 1931 is to provide visitors with a brief outline of the history and principal features of each type of monument in the area covered by the guide. Almost all the work of conservation and improvement of amenities in connection with these monuments has been carried out since the close of the Great European War. It has been the policy of my Department, while deliberately avoiding restoration or rebuilding, to preserve such monuments as have been committed to its care in a manner more worthy of their national importance and historic interest. It has been our aim to make the monuments as intelligible as possible to the ordinary visitor. Individual guide books, the work of experts, for each of the more important monuments either have been published or are in course of preparation. Plans showing successive building dates are included in these monographs and are displayed in frames at the monuments. The Department's custodians have instructions not only to maintain the amenities of the monuments but also to assist visitors with such information as they are able to give.

These regional guides are accordingly designed to supplement the more detailed archæological data available by a more general and popular account of all the monuments in a group of counties. It is hoped that they will enable the visitor to know what other monuments exist in the neighbourhood of any one he may happen to visit, and to place any individual monument in its historical setting in relation to other monuments of a similar kind.

The story of our past is written not only in history books but in stone. But quite apart from their appeal to our historical sense, many of our monuments are great works of art, the legacy of wonderful craftsmen in successive ages.

Until recently, the popular idea of ruins was that they should be picturesque and preferably ivy-clad. To-day, with the advance of knowledge, people want to learn more about the ruins, and to study the styles of building and ornament that may be found in them, without, in most cases, being troubled by the jargon of technical terms. Some of the latter are inevitable even in a popular guide. But in the main, this first of the proposed series of regional guides is written primarily for amateurs, and its production will be justified if it can add to the numbers of those who enjoy and take a pride in our national heritage.

W. ORMSBY GORE

PREFACE TO THE THIRD EDITION

This series of guides to the Ancient Monuments of Great Britain under the care of the Ministry of Works was designed by Lord Harlech, and began to be published under his inspiration, when he was the Rt. Hon. W. Ormsby-Gore, M.P., and First Commissioner of Works. He himself wrote the first three volumes, on Northern, Southern and Central England, which were issued in 1935-8. The fifth volume on North Wales, also written by him, was published in 1948. During the war, inevitably, the earlier volumes went out of print, and the stocks were destroyed by enemy action. A new edition is therefore now issued, brought up to date with the author's consent by the inclusion of additional monuments taken over since 1939, and by some revision in cases where the discovery of new evidence has led to a modification of previous theories. With these exceptions, however, the text in each case remains substantially that of the original author.

The Ancient Monuments and Historic Buildings of Britain suffered remarkably little damage from enemy action during the war, but those in the custody of the Ministry of Works suffered from the transference of the skilled men who maintained them to other work of national importance. The Ancient Monuments

Division has thus six years' arrears of work to overtake, and it has to build up again its expert staff without taking men from work where they are more urgently required. At some of the monuments work has been suspended, at others it is being carried on with a reduced staff, and at many which have been taken over since 1939 it has not yet been possible to start the work of preservation.

The Ancient Monuments Division is now once more active all over the country and its work is being gradually extended, and this series of guide books is accordingly now re-issued, to stimulate again the interest of the public in these treasures of our national heritage.

CHARLES W. KEY,

Ministry of Works *Minister of Works*

January, 1949

NOTE.—*The names of monuments which are Crown property or in the guardianship of the Ministry of Works are printed in italics.*

PREHISTORIC PERIOD

The long glacial epoch that probably terminated in Britain about 8000 B.C. drove out our pre-glacial fauna. In northern England a few tops of the Pennines and of the Cleveland Moors may have stood above the all-embracing covering of ice. The Kirkdale cave in the Vale of Pickering has yielded the bones of the hyena, hippopotamus, lion, straight-tusked elephant, and the slender-nosed rhinoceros, evidence of the pre-glacial animals of our country.

In its retreat the glacier deposited between Tadcaster on the Wharfe and a point just south of York on the Ouse a great terminal moraine or bank of stones across the Vale of York, which in the subsequent "Atlantic" period, when the climate was warm and very wet, proved the one possible highway through the swamp and dense forest from Wharfedale to the Wolds available to Neolithic and Early Bronze Age man.

Palæolithic man of the so-called Cresswell Crag culture seems to have hung on to a miserable existence on the edges of the ice through the last glacial epoch, and even to have survived into the succeeding warm period. During this—the Mesolithic—age, hunters and fishermen from across the North Sea reached our north-eastern coasts. They were very primitive folk, ignorant of agriculture and of domestic animals, and it was not until the third millennium before Christ that we find the evidence of occupation of settled cultures in the East Yorkshire Wolds, continuing there successively till Roman times. The Yorkshire coast appears to have been one of the chief lines of entry of wave after wave of invading settlement for the three thousand years before the Norman Conquest.

There are many reasons why the first agricultural settlers in Britain selected the chalk downs and wolds as their dwelling places, but the main reason was climatic. The dry " Boreal " climate had given way to the wet "Atlantic," and much of Lowland Britain consisted of forest or marsh. The heath and peat uplands were water-logged in winter and, with the means at Neolithic man's disposal, uncultivable and irreclaimable. Only the chalk and the limestone gave him the means of existence, and the former contained the most essential raw material for his weapons and implements, namely flint.

Plate 1. THE ROMAN WALL WEST OF HOUSESTEADS.

Plate 2. WHEELDALE MOOR. THE ROMAN ROAD.

Plate 3. CORBRIDGE ROMAN STATION. THE GRANARIES.

Plate 4. BYLAND ABBEY. SOUTH TRANSEPT.

In the East Yorkshire uplands the remains of no fewer than twenty-five long barrows are known as against only one west of the Vale of York. Whenever measurable, the skulls found in these long barrows are long and narrow. The long barrows were communal burial places, the bones (usually partly burnt) of many individuals being found in them. With them are found leaf- or lozenge-shaped flint arrow heads, flint axes with rounded butts, flint knives and numerous sherds of smooth, black round-bottomed pottery.

Similar barrows occur in the Lincolnshire Wolds, the Cotswolds, Wiltshire, Dorset, Hampshire and Sussex. These long-headed, long-barrow people are the first of our direct ancestors who can be called civilized, and many of them came from Western Europe, probably from Spain and Portugal. They cultivated wheat, had domestic animals, showed remarkable skill in making their neolithic implements and round-bottomed pottery, and were the first to move large stones in connection with the ritual of their burying places. They lived on chalk uplands, hunted the wild red deer, and avoided the forest-clad lowlands. Their characteristic long barrows seem to be completely absent from Cumberland and Northumberland.

This long-barrow civilization probably reached East Yorkshire late in its history, towards 2000 B.C., and was followed by the invasion of the round-headed " beaker " folk who probably reached Yorkshire from Holland and Germany, round about 1900 B.C., and settled in the same sites. Their beakers or drinking vessels were made of a fine, light-coloured pottery, had a pronounced waist slightly above their middle height, and flat bottoms. Over 150 or about one-third of the total number of complete beakers found in England have been found in Yorkshire, and of these more than 130 came from the Wolds. A few beaker sherds have been found near the Northumberland coast, and the beaker culture certainly spread to parts of Cumberland. At first the beaker folk were still in the neolithic stage, but during their dominance the first bronze implements —daggers and flat axes—were introduced by trade, probably from the Spanish peninsula. In addition to flint axes, they used in Yorkshire polished stone axes of a volcanic ash greenstone from Borrowdale in Cumberland. More than half the polished stone axes (other than flint) found in the Wolds are of this material, and the Cumberland beakers are identical in form with the Yorkshire Wold beakers.

Perhaps the most remarkable and important Early Bronze Age beaker burial known was found at Kellythorpe Farm, near Driffield (East Riding). It consisted of the skeleton of a tall man buried in a crouching position with knees doubled up under the chin and arms crossed. When found the skeleton still had the fragmentary remains of a woven shroud. Behind the waist was a small plain bronze dagger and fragments of its wooden handle and sheath. At his neck were three large conical amber beads (of Baltic origin). On his right forearm (he must have been left-handed) was a Cumbrian greenstone wristguard to protect his wrist from the recoil of the bow-string, attached by means of a leather arm-band studded with three gold-headed studs (probably of Irish origin). Above his knees was the skeleton of the head of a hawk, and behind the feet a characteristic " beaker " 7 inches high. Had there been in addition some tanged and barbed flint arrow heads, this would have been the ideally complete Early Bronze Age beaker burial.

In the course of time the original form of beaker was gradually replaced in burials by a modified local type, and later by the wider and squatter " food vessel," which seems to represent a new element in the population. More than two hundred and fifty of these " food vessels " have been found in the Yorkshire Wolds, and over sixty on the Cleveland Hills. The number and variety of bronze implements increased in this period as well as the trade in gold. The latter without much doubt came from Ireland, and one of the trade routes between Ireland and the Continent can be established by the finds of flat bronze axes and gold lunulæ. It appears to have been up the Ribble and its tributary the Calder past Nelson and Colne, through the Aire Gap to Skipton, and so by Ilkley and Otley to the York moraine ; thence up Garrowby Hill to the Wolds and across the North Sea from ports on either side of Flamborough Head to Denmark and North Germany. This and the Stainmore Pass route into Cumberland were the two earliest prehistoric trade routes across the Pennines.

The food-vessel folk gradually took to cremating instead of interring their dead, and developed a characteristic form of large cinerary urn in which their ashes and calcined bones were placed under round barrows. Over 450 such large urns have been found in Yorkshire, and in this period man began effective descent from the uplands into the Vale of York. We have every reason to believe that after the comparatively wet period of Neolithic and Early Bronze Age times the climate of Britain became much drier and so remained until a renewal of wetter and Atlantic-type conditions in the Early Iron Age. In the West Tanfield-Boroughbridge area definite association has been established between these urn burials and the flanged axe of the Bronze Age, six examples of the wide-flanged type coming from this area alone. Neither copper nor tin has ever been found in Yorkshire and all bronze implements must have been traded from a distance. With these cinerary-urn folk we have reached the Middle Bronze Age, probably about 1400 B.C.

The Late Bronze Age is attested in Yorkshire by the discovery, often in hoards, of looped and socketed axes of north Alpine type and the introduction of the first bronze swords ; new types of bronze spear head also appear. Late Bronze Age finds in Yorkshire are commonest near the coast and throughout Holderness, and seem to point to trade with north-west Germany if not to an actual invasion from that quarter. No late Bronze Age implements have been found in Yorkshire barrows or in any sites connected with the cinerary-urn folk, who are unknown in Holderness. Some of the newcomers very likely lived in pile dwellings in marshy country.

In 1926 on the *Castle Hill* at *Scarborough* an important occupation of socket-axe folk was discovered in definite association with pottery of Hallstatt type (so-called from the famous necropolis in Upper Austria), which has been found elsewhere in England, notably at Hengistbury Head on the Hampshire coast, and near Devizes in Wiltshire. With the characteristic Hallstatt pottery and the bronze objects at Scarborough an iron pin was also found.

The later Hallstatt culture, with its use of iron, was introduced into Southern England by a series of immigrants in the sixth and fifth centuries B.C. In the north these immigrations are less clearly defined, and, though the Scarborough site belongs to the sixth century, there seems to have been no very general immigration of Iron Age peoples for some three centuries.

It is probable that the Hallstatt folk were Celtic in speech, and that of their successors was definitely Celtic, or Brythonic. The latter buried their chieftains in chariots, and their culture was that known as La Tène (from the famous settlements on the Lake of Neuchâtel in Switzerland). Their continental links are with the Marne and Middle Seine in Gaul, and thence with La

Tène itself. On the Yorkshire Wolds they can be confidently identified with the Parisii of the geographer Ptolemy, and the date of their invasion may be put in the latter half of the third century B.C. They colonized East Yorkshire, and their influence spread in the following centuries over the highlands of the Pennines, where they seem to have established their rule over the indigenous peoples, and so to have formed the confederacy known to the Romans as the Brigantes. It has been suggested by archæologists that the name "Brigantes" is of Swiss origin.

I have omitted from this story of the succession of prehistoric civilization in the northern counties, chiefly in East Yorkshire, any reference to the megalithic monuments which, in the popular mind at any rate, are the best-known remains of our prehistoric peoples. Curiously these are fairly numerous in Cumberland and Westmorland, especially in the form of large stone circles, which are unknown in Yorkshire. The best-known megaliths in Yorkshire are the great monolith at Rudston in the East Riding and the three "Devil's Arrows" near Boroughbridge. These latter are large monoliths (two of them 22 and the other 18 feet high) erected in "a line" north and south at intervals of nearly 100 yards. They are made of millstone grit from near Knaresborough and, standing in an area where Middle Bronze Age cinerary-urn burials are frequent, probably date from that age.

As to the age and purpose of the Cumbrian megalithic circles we are still quite in the dark. Excavation at *Avebury*, in Wiltshire, has proved that the megalithic avenue leading to the great circle is definitely assignable to the age of the beaker folk when still in the stage of neolithic culture before bronze was known to them, at any rate in that area. It was therefore erected about 1800 B.C.

There are at least four megalithic stone circles in Cumberland whose size is such that they were probably religious or ceremonial meeting places. The best known is at *Castlerigg*, near Keswick, with a diameter of approximately 100 feet. Similar circles are at Swinside, near Broughton, and in Eskdale. The latter is approximately 100 feet in diameter, almost exactly the same size as the Keswick circle, and contains within it five small round barrows, each with a colonnade or peristalith of stones round their bases. But by far the largest and most remarkable is "Long Meg and her Daughters" near Little Salkeld, about

7 miles north-east of Penrith. This circle ranks fourth in importance in England as a whole, after *Avebury*, *Stonehenge* and *Stanton Drew*.

Long Meg and her Daughters consists of a circle of sixty-four stones, measuring 360 feet on its longer axis due east and west, and 305 feet on its shorter axis due north and south. Outside the circle (if we may use the word) stands Long Meg, the tallest stone of all, due south-west of the crossing point of the axes. On this stone has been a curious small cup mark surrounded by two concentric circles. The other two stones outside the circle, one of which is still standing, form a sort of gateway situated between south-west and south. The stones vary very much in size. The smaller ones are apparently unhewn, but most of the larger ones seem to have been shaped in a very similar manner to the broader stones in the *West Kennet Avenue* at *Avebury*. In addition, these shaped stones show signs of having been dressed on the inner side.

The great circle of Shap in Westmorland, of which Stukeley's record in the early eighteenth century exists, appears to have had an accompanying megalithic avenue leading down to the river Lowther. Half the inner circle remains close to the railway line, and a few stones of the avenue can be seen. We are still uncertain regarding the purpose and date or dates of the megalithic circles and avenues which are such a feature of the prehistoric remains in Britain and, to all intents and purposes, of no other country except Brittany. Further scientific excavation of such circles as *Stanton Drew* in Somerset, Long Meg and her Daughters in Cumberland, and *Callernish* in the Island of Lewis may yet reveal their secrets. For the time being we can only reject their present popular and quite unscientific ascription to the Druids, the " Brahmins " of the latest arrivals among the Celtic tribes found in Central Gaul and Britain by the Romans. This ascription is due to the eighteenth-century archæologist Stukeley, and rests solely on his lively imagination. More probably the megalithic idea was first introduced by the long-barrow people, and was continued and developed by the beaker folk.

ROMAN PERIOD

At the time of the coming of the Romans to Britain in A.D. 43 most of Northern England was occupied by the Brigantes and by the more cultured Parisii in Holderness and the Wolds. With the Brigantes the Romans came to terms, and it was their Queen Cartimandua who surrendered Caractacus to them when he had fled to her for refuge. For thirty years the Brigantes remained independent, though distracted by civil war, in which Rome from time to time intervened. But in about A.D. 73 the Roman conquest of the north of England began. The IX Legion was then based on Lincoln, whence a military road was pushed northward to the Humber, which was crossed by a ferry to Brough, and thence northward along the western base of the Wolds to Malton. Roman vessels, as Vikings' vessels later, could navigate the Ouse as far as York, and about A.D. 75 York became the depot of the IX Legion. York Minster to-day occupies what was approximately the centre of the original Roman fortress.

From A.D. 78 to 85 Agricola was Governor of Britain and from the terse pages of his son-in-law Tacitus as well as from the contemporary archæological evidence we can deduce the history of his great campaigns, first in North Wales and then into Scotland. After dealing with the Welsh, Agricola built and " fortified " his new roads from Chester to Ribchester on the Ribble, thence following the prehistoric route through the Aire gap and Ilkley to *Aldborough*, which became a Roman town under the name of Isurium Brigantum. Similarly, from Ribchester the Roman road was pushed due north through Lancaster, Tebay, Crosby Ravensworth to Carlisle. Professor Haverfield attributed to Agricola the construction of the Roman road from York through *Aldborough* to Cataractonium (the modern Catterick, once again a camp), thence to *Corstopitum*, near Corbridge on the Tyne, and thence to Newstead on the Tweed. From just north of Cataractonium another road along another well-defined prehistoric route crossed the Stainmore Pass to Carlisle and is still the modern motorist's highway to Scotland.

Agricola also constructed a road with some intervening forts upon it from Carlisle to *Corstopitum*, some few miles south of the line later followed by Hadrian's Wall (Plate 1). The scanty remnants of Agricola's road are known to-day as the " Stanegate." Agricola's advance into Scotland was probably from *Corstopitum* up Redesdale to Jedburgh.

In the first years of the second century the Brigantes, allied with the Northern Caledonians, rose in revolt, and the Roman possessions in Scotland were lost. The frontier was temporarily stabilized on the line of Agricola's Stanegate, and some new forts were built near this road. In the course of this revolt the IX Legion at York was annihilated, and was replaced by the VI Legion from the Lower Rhine. In A.D. 121 the Emperor Hadrian arrived in person to avenge the Roman defeat. He decided to establish a definite frontier to the Empire from the Tyne to the Solway, and to him and his legate, the governor, Aulus Platorius Nepos, we owe the construction of the great Wall that still bears the Emperor's name. In about A.D. 145 the Emperor Antoninus Pius reconquered the Lowlands of Scotland, and a new frontier-line was established from the Forth to the Clyde. Hadrian's Wall, however, was still manned.

For fifty years this state of affairs continued, until in 196 Clodius Albinus, governor of Britain, denuded the province of troops, to fight for the throne of the Empire against Septimius Severus. He was defeated and slain at Lyons in Gaul, and the northern parts of Britain were invaded by the barbarians who ravaged and destroyed as far south as the legionary fortresses of York and Chester. The governor appointed by Septimius Severus had to buy off the invaders. However, in 208 Severus himself came to Britain and re-established the authority of Rome, penetrating far into Scotland. He did not, however, reoccupy the Lowlands, but restored and strengthened the defences of Hadrian's Wall, which thus became again the frontier. He died at York in 211. The land had peace for seventy-seven years till the rebellion of Carausius, who commanded the Roman fleet in Britain, and established himself as a semi-independent Emperor. On his assassination the Wall was again overrun, to be restored again by Constantius Chlorus in 296. He too died in York in 305. Again there was a long peace till the renewed disasters of 367, and it was only partially restored by Theodosius in 370. In 395 Stilicho cleared the province that had been ravaged by invaders by land and sea, but in 402 on account of the desperate situation in Italy he recalled the legion from York, and in 410 the usurper Con-

stantine III in his gamble for the throne withdrew the last
Roman garrisons and they never returned. Thereafter for more
than 150 years history is silent, until Aella, the first recorded
Anglian King of Deira (Yorkshire), reigned in 585. In the west
there is evidence in the sixth century of the somewhat shadowy
Celtic Kingdom of Strathclyde, stretching from the Clyde west
of the Pennines to the Mersey, till it was overwhelmed by the
Anglian King of Bernicia (Northumberland). The capital of
this Celtic Kingdom of Strathclyde was probably at Dumbarton.

Such in outline is the story. Of the monuments there is
none more striking or romantic than the great Wall itself.

It was built for a length of 73½ English miles from Wallsend,
near Tynemouth, to Bowness on Solway. At its highest point
on the moors it reached an elevation of 1,230 feet above sea-level.
It was faced with squared blocks of stone and surmounted, no
doubt, by battlements, and was cleverly sited so as to give it all
possible advantages of ground as a defensive position against
the north. At intervals of from three to seven miles along the
Wall are twenty-three forts or " castella," the permanent
quarters of the garrison troops. These forts were fitted into the
actual Wall, and their position, scale and lay-out can still be
clearly seen at *Housesteads* (Borcovicium) on one of the best
preserved sections of the Wall, and at *Chesters* (Cilurnum).

In addition to these larger forts there was at every Roman
mile (1,618 yards) along the Wall a small fort about 55 feet by
70 feet, capable of accommodating about 50 men. These small
forts are known as " Milecastles," and between them there were
two square stone turrets in each mile. These milecastles and
turrets accommodated the men who carried out the actual
patrol duty along the Wall.

Archæologists have numbered the milecastles from east to
west, and the turrets are lettered a and b after the number
of the milecastle to the east of them.

South of the Wall runs the line of earthwork known as the
" Vallum," which was clearly part of the scheme, though its
precise purpose is still obscure. It consisted of a ditch about
30 feet wide and 7 feet deep, steep-sided and flat-bottomed, with
a bank on either side. Where it crossed a steep ravine its sides
were sometimes revetted with stone. It was constructed as far
as possible in a straight line without regard to the defensive
advantages of the ground, consequently, its distance from the
Wall varies. It has not been found east of Newcastle. At

Benwell a causeway crossing the Vallum to give access to the Fort to the north of it is preserved by the Ministry of Works, in the middle of a housing estate, and in the next street the Ministry also maintains the foundations of a small temple of the otherwise unknown gods Anociticus and Antenociticus.

Three Roman stone bridges were constructed, across the Tyne at Pons Ælius (Newcastle) and Corbridge, and across the North Tyne at Chollerford. Much of these bridges remained till the great flood of the year 1771, and fragments of that at Corbridge can still be seen when the river is low. At Chollerford the eastern abutment of the bridge is now in the guardianship of the Ministry of Works.

Corstopitum near Corbridge was originally one of Agricola's forts : then, during the operations in Scotland in the second century, it became a military town and supply depot. It has been suggested that Severus intended to move a legion there : if so, the idea was abandoned on his death, but *Corstopitum* remained an important military base, and a considerable civilian settlement developed there also.

Corstopitum lies about $2\frac{1}{2}$ miles south of the Wall, and from it the main road ran south through Catterick to York. It was extensively excavated in 1907-14, and mostly covered in again. Between the two wars it was being opened up once more by the Ministry of Works, which owns a large part of this most important site. This work has now been resumed. Most of the buildings now exposed date from the period of Septimius Severus (circa A.D. 210) but were considerably altered a hundred years later under Constantius. The principal structures to be seen are first two large granaries with buttressed walls, flagged floors and elaborate basement ventilation, having the remains of a portico of columns along their southern front. (Plate 3.) East of these is a fountain, with considerable remains of the aqueduct which brought the water in from the north. East of the fountain is a large building, enclosing a courtyard about 175 feet square. This was perhaps designed for the headquarters of the Legion which Severus may have intended to move here, but it was never finished. It was evidently to have been of a monumental character, and the surviving fragments of its walls of rusticated blocks are among the most impressive of Roman buildings in Britain. To the south of this are the remains of two military compounds, which were joined into one in the fourth century. There are also the foundations of several small temples and of shops. The Museum on the site is maintained by the Trustees of the Corbridge Excavation Fund, and contains most of the objects found in the diggings since 1907. There is a particularly good series of inscriptions, much interesting but mainly rather crude sculpture including the famous " Corbridge Lion," and a very complete collection of pottery, bronze objects, etc. The coins extend over practically the whole range of the Roman occupation of Britain, and include a second-century hoard of 160 gold pieces, electrotypes of which are displayed.

In addition to the Wall, the Romans maintained till nearly the end of the fourth century at least five advanced forts north of the Wall, at High Rochester, and Risingham in Redesdale, connected with *Corstopitum* by a military road, at Bewcastle in north-east Cumberland, connected by a road with the Wall fort at *Camboglanna* (Birdoswald), at Netherby in Eskdale and at Birrens, near Ecclefechan.

From the time of Hadrian onwards three Legions were maintained in Britain—namely, the second (Augusta) stationed at Caerleon, the sixth (Victrix) at York and the twentieth (Valeria Victrix) at Chester. These Legions, each of over 5,000 men of all arms, were composed entirely of Roman citizens, and were highly trained and heavily armed. Each Legion lived and acted as a unit, but detachments (vexillationes) were often sent away for particular duties. Such detachments figure often in the inscriptions at Corbridge.

Except in times of active operations the actual garrisoning of the Wall was carried out not by legionaries but by " auxiliaries," organized into " cohorts " of infantry and " alæ " of cavalry, under Roman officers. Legionaries as well as auxiliaries were drawn from all parts of the Empire. Of the many memorials of life on the Wall that have been unearthed none is more eloquent than the inscribed votive stones and altars dedicated by individual soldiers to Mars, to Jupiter, to Mithras, etc. Near each fort, with its prætorium (commanding officer's house) and barracks, there grew up dependent villages inhabited by the wives, camp-followers and traders. Public baths and other evidences of amenity were erected. It is perhaps on Hadrian's Wall even more than in Rome itself that we can be impressed with the might and majesty of the Roman Empire, the loyalty it inspired and the degrees of organization and authority that it attained for several centuries. The Wall is the silent witness, in many ways the most remarkable in all Europe, of one of the greatest endeavours of human history.

The greatest destruction of the Wall took place after the Jacobite Rising in 1745. That Prince Charlie ever got so far south as Derby was due to the fact that there was then no adequate road for George II's army and artillery across the Pennines from Yorkshire or Northumberland. Accordingly, when Prince Charlie had been defeated, a proper road from Newcastle to Carlisle was ordered to be made by an Act of Parliament passed in 1751. For much of its length this new road was built on and of the Roman Wall, but for a few miles just west of Newcastle it was sited just to the north of it, and some pieces of the Wall are still standing. The most easterly, just east of Denton Burn, is in the custody of the Corporation of Newcastle upon Tyne. On the top of the rise west of the Burn is a stretch of 70 yards, which is in the guardianship of the Ministry of Works : this includes *Denton Hall Turret* (No. 7b) ; a little further west some more pieces of the Wall were recently revealed by road-widening operations and are now preserved by the Ministry. Four miles further west, at *Heddon-on-the-Wall*, a length of 280 yards is in the Ministry's care. Some 15 miles further west, where the road swings north of the Wall to descend into the valley of the North Tyne, two short pieces have been handed over to the Ministry of Works since the last war, one at *Planetrees Farm*, on the top of the bank, and the other at the edge of the grounds of *Brunton House*, near the bottom. This latter piece includes Turret No. 26b. As stated above, the eastern land-abutment of the bridge by which the Wall crossed the North Tyne is also now in the Ministry's care. West of *Chesters* (Chollerford) the road returns to the line of the Wall generally for the next six miles, but near *Sewingshields Farm* it finally swings to the south, and the Wall continues along the line of the whinstone crags through desolate moorland country. The Ministry of Works has recently been made guardian of a stretch of over two Roman miles of the Wall starting from the point where road and Wall part company. This stretch includes milecastles Nos. 34 and 35, and five Turrets, Nos. 33b to 35b, but unfortunately very little of the masonry survives along here since it was sold for road-repairs in the early nineteenth century. The great fort of *Housesteads* (Borcovicium) and a length of the Wall to the west of it are the property of the National Trust,

and it is in this region that the best stretches of Wall are preserved, and that there are the best views of the wild land to the
north. The highest piece of the Wall, on *Winshields Crags*, is
in the custody of the Ministry of Works, including Milecastle
No. 40. Five miles further west, on *Walltown Crags* near
Greenhead, a fine stretch of Wall (including Turret No. 45a)
was saved from destruction by the action of the then Office of
Works in 1939, but during the war the urgent demand for
road-metal led to the destruction by quarrying of over 300
yards of Wall just east of this point. This, however, has now
been stopped, and no more of the Wall will be destroyed, since
the best parts are now subject to a Preservation Scheme under
the Ancient Monuments Acts.

Just over the Cumberland border, where the Newcastle
and Carlisle Railway crosses the line of the Wall, the Ministry of
Works has the guardianship of *Poltross Burn Milecastle* (No. 48),
and the next two miles of the Wall westward are also in its care.
This stretch includes the very good piece in the Vicarage garden
at *Gilsland*, Turrets Nos. 48a and 48b, and the most interesting
eastern abutment of the bridge by which the Wall crossed the
river Irthing at *Willowford*. It also includes *Harrow's Scar
Milecastle* (No. 49) on top of the cliff opposite *Willowford*, and
the Wall westward from it to the great fort of Birdoswald
(*Camboglanna*), the outer walls of which are also in the Ministry's
care, together with 500 yards of the Wall beyond it to the west.
Three miles west *Banks East Turret* (No. 52a) with a short piece
of Wall is also in the Ministry's charge.

No other part of the Wall is in the Ministry's guardianship,
but it has the custody of one other important Roman work
which is part of the Wall system, namely the fort of Chesterholm
(*Vindolanda*). This fort lies some two miles south of the Wall
on Agricola's road, the Stanegate, but it was incorporated in the
defensive system of the Wall. The parts exposed are the walls
and gates, and the Headquarters building (principia), which
all show the drastic reconstruction which took place in the
early fourth century. Further reconstruction took place after
the general Theodosius had restored the Wall frontier after the
great disaster of 367. Just outside the fort a Roman milestone
is preserved *in situ* beside the Roman road. South of the Wall,
the whole of northern Britain was covered with a network of
strategic roads, with forts at intervals along them. Three of the
mediæval castles which are in the guardianship of the Ministry

of Works in this area are sited within Roman forts, namely *Bowes*, *Brough* and *Brougham*. At the last some interesting Roman inscriptions are preserved, but the only visible traces of the forts are the grassy banks of their ramparts.

In the North Riding of Yorkshire, on the moors north of Pickering, are the interesting Roman Camps at Cawthorn. These were only temporary camps and are a survival of the early years of the Roman conquest of the north, and date from the last quarter of the first century. These camps are not in the Ministry's care, but some four miles to the north, in the wild country on *Wheeldale Moor*, a stretch of a mile of paved Roman road is preserved under the guardianship of the Ministry of Works (Plate 2). This road also probably dates originally from the first century, but may well have been repaired and reconditioned in the fourth. From the end of the third century onwards, the Romans in Britain had to protect their province not only from the threat beyond the Wall but from the Teutonic invaders by sea. Farther south they protected the coast by a series of great fortresses on what was known as the " Saxon Shore " between the Wash and Spithead, of which *Portchester* at the head of Portsmouth harbour is now the most striking. On the Yorkshire coast they established a series of coastguard or signal stations in the latter part of the fourth century. One such station is still to be seen on the *Castle Hill* at *Scarborough*.

Whereas in the rest of England the Roman occupation was civil and commercial, in the north it was throughout chiefly military. There were, however, civil sites as well. The flourishing Roman colony of York, side by side with the legionary fortress, had a vigorous civil life of which copious traces are to be seen in the Museum of the Yorkshire Philosophical Society in that city. The Brigantes too were organized by the Romans into a community with local self-government, the centre of which was at *Aldborough*, near Boroughbridge. This seems to have been a purely Roman foundation, having no continuity with the earlier occupation. There were also several villas in the Vale of York, and in the East Riding, especially in the neighbourhood of the fort at Malton. When the Roman armies were withdrawn in the early fifth century, this civil life was left, if not unorganized, at least largely defenceless against the attacks of Picts and Scots from the North, and Angles and Saxons (chiefly the former) from overseas. But for the brief daylight of the Christian kingdom of the Angles in Northumbria, it was not until the Norman Conquest that the North recovered sufficient civilization to leave behind enduring monuments in the way of stone buildings of any size.

MEDIÆVAL PERIOD

It has been possible so far to relate the monuments to brief historical surveys, but, now that the mediæval period has been reached with its manifold developments in religious and secular architecture and art, it will be more convenient to readers to depart from this plan. The mediæval monuments will be dealt with under the two main heads, ecclesiastical and secular, and, instead of a history illustrated by the archæological remains, so much will be given by way of historical introduction as is necessary to an understanding of the individual monuments.

MONASTIC REMAINS

The northern counties are justly famous for their monastic ruins, the abbeys and priories of Yorkshire alone exceeding in number and magnificence those of any other county in England. In our region the Ministry of Works is now the guardian of seventeen structures, including some of the finest. These are the Benedictine abbey of *Whitby* and the Benedictine priories of *Lindisfarne*, *Tynemouth* and *Finchale*; the Cistercian abbeys of *Rievaulx*, *Byland*, *Roche*, *Salley* and *Furness*; the Præmonstratensian abbeys of *Easby*, *Shap* and *Egglestone*; the Augustinian priories of *Lanercost*, *Kirkham* and *Gisborough*; the Cluniac priory of *Monk Bretton*, near Barnsley; and, finally, the very remarkable Carthusian house of *Mount Grace*, near Northallerton.

The most important monastic ruins not in the custody of the Ministry are the Cistercian abbeys of Fountains, Kirkstall and Jervaulx, and the Benedictine abbey of St. Mary at York. Apart from ruins, the splendid Benedictine abbey of Selby, and the fine Augustinian priories of Hexham, Brinkburn, Bridlington, Bolton in Wharfedale and Cartmel are still in use as parish churches.

In addition to the historical and architectural interest of the actual buildings it would be difficult to find anywhere in Europe a more romantic ruin than *Lindisfarne* (Plate 12) or one in a more splendid setting than the incomparable *Rievaulx* (Plate 7).

The first attempt to Christianize pagan Northumbria was made by Paulinus, a follower of St. Augustine, early in the seventh century, but this effort was followed by a pagan reaction, and the evangelization of the North was due to the mission of St. Aidan from Iona in the reign of King, afterwards Saint, Oswald in A.D. 635. St. Aidan became the first Abbot-Bishop of Holy Island (*Lindisfarne*). The story of this famous monastic see is illuminated by the career of the sixth Abbot-Bishop, St. Cuthbert, who was first buried in the place of honour on the right of the High Altar of Lindisfarne. When the pagan Vikings descended upon Holy Island in A.D. 875 and destroyed the monastery, the monks removed his body elsewhere, and finally, in the tenth century, it found a resting-place at Durham, where the Norman Bishops erected the present great cathedral in his honour. The excavations on Holy Island undertaken by the then Office of Works have brought to light a number of stone crosses and name-stones dating for the most part from the Anglian period (A.D. 675-875), now preserved in the small museum on the site. But of artistic products the most famous is the Lindisfarne gospels, the superb illuminated manuscript of the early years of the eighth century, which is one of the chief treasures of the British Museum.

The flowering period of Anglian art was short. It may have begun with the arrival of Theodore of Tarsus from Byzantine lands, but more probably it was due to the introduction of Italian craftsmen by St. Benedict Biscop, the founder of the monasteries of Jarrow and Wearmouth in the last quarter of the seventh century. It continued through the first half of the eighth century and then decayed, being finally overwhelmed by the Viking invasions in the ninth century. It produced in illuminated manuscripts and sculptured reliefs most remarkable works of art, blending the age-old traditions of La Tène Celtic ornament with Mediterranean motifs, and may well have been the cause rather than the consequence of the artistic revival in Ireland between the late eighth and eleventh centuries. The High Cross of Bewcastle still *in situ* in the most northerly parish churchyard in Cumberland, inscribed with Runic letters, contains motifs such as the vine scroll which must be of Mediterranean origin. The similar fragments of the Easby Abbey cross in the Victoria and Albert Museum bear traces of the same cultural influences. The cross at Irton in South Cumberland also dates from the eighth century. These earlier High Crosses of Northumbria are quite distinct from the tenth and eleventh-century wheel-head crosses of the Christianized Viking period. Perhaps the finest of these Viking crosses is that at Gosforth in Cumberland.

The most important and extensive remains of an Early Anglian monastery of so-called Celtic type are those which were excavated alongside the later Benedictine abbey ruins of *Whitby* (Plate 8). This Abbey of Streoneshalh was founded and ruled by St. Hilda, a great-niece of King Aecfrith of Northumbria, in A.D. 657. Excavation revealed the foundations of many cells and oratories in which important finds were made, such as gilt bronze ornaments with openwork interlacing patterns. This monastery produced at least two notable sons before it was ruthlessly destroyed by the Vikings, in A.D. 870. First we may mention Caedmon, a name which suggests Celtic rather than Anglian blood, who was the first English poet. The other was St. John of Beverley, over whose shrine still rises the great church of Beverley Minster.

Anglian civilization under the Kings of Northumbria extended both sides of the Border and reached a higher level of culture than any other part of Britain in the seventh, eighth and early half of the ninth century. It was shattered by the Vikings, invasions of Danes, Norwegians, and Icelanders who first destroyed and then colonized the northern counties. To the Vikings we owe the division of Yorkshire into " ridings " and " wapentakes," and the numerous place names ending in " by ", " thwaite " and " scale." It was owing to the Angles and the Vikings that the Scottish Lowlands lost their predominantly Celtic character.

Though the Vikings were gradually Christianized, their inroads lasted till the Norman Conquest. Harold Hadrada, the Landwaster, of Norway met defeat and death at Stamford Bridge from Harold, the Saxon King of England, in 1066, and it was this battle that so weakened the military strength of the Saxon host, that it enabled William of Normandy to achieve the victory of Hastings a few weeks later.

The Norman Conquerors built abbeys and cathedrals as well as castles. The Conqueror himself founded the Abbey of

Plate 5. KIRKHAM PRIORY. THE GATEHOUSE.

Plate 6.   FURNESS ABBEY.   EAST SIDE OF CLOISTER.

Plate 7.   RIEVAULX ABBEY.

Plate 8. WHITBY ABBEY. THE QUIRE.

Plate 9.   LANERCOST PRIORY.

Plate 10.   EASBY ABBEY.   REFECTORY, FROM THE SOUTH.

Plate 11.   TYNEMOUTH PRIORY.   EAST END.

Plate 12.   LINDISFARNE PRIORY.   INTERIOR OF CHURCH, LOOKING WEST.

Selby, and made the Bishops of Durham, who were *ex officio* Abbots of the Benedictine Cathedral Monastery, Counts Palatine of the North.

The Norman priories of *Lindisfarne* and *Finchale* rose as cells of the Cathedral Monastery of Durham, the former built, no doubt, by the same craftsmen who erected the great naves of Durham and Dunfermline, those revolutionary craftsmen who were the first to throw a " ribbed " stone vault over a great nave ; it was completed by 1133.

To the Benedictines of Durham is due the re-establishment of monastic buildings on the old Anglian site at *Tynemouth*, but their foundation was short-lived owing to quarrels with Robert de Mowbray, the Norman Earl of Northumberland. The latter expelled the Durham monks and gave the site to the Abbey of St. Alban in Hertfordshire. *Tynemouth Priory* (Plate 11) remained a cell of St. Alban's till the dissolution. The erection of the present church was begun in 1085. The body of Malcolm Canmore, King of Scotland, who had fallen at Alnwick, was buried in Tynemouth in 1093 and the bones of St. Oswin were translated there in 1110. The existing remains of the Norman church are but scanty, though we still possess much of the additions at the east and west ends made about the year 1200. Similarly at *Whitby* little remains of the Norman building, but much of the magnificent thirteenth-century Gothic choir still stands.

To King Henry I we owe the introduction into England of the order of the Augustinian canons regular, and Carlisle, a new see created by Henry I, is interesting as being the only English cathedral that was served by Augustinian canons.

It is to this northern Augustinian influence that we owe the great churches of Hexham, *Lanercost* and Brinkburn, all of them admirable examples of the first pointed arch style of the end of the twelfth and beginning of the thirteenth century. All have one special peculiarity. The naves were built with only one aisle, on the north side, with a north porch, for the accommodation of the local laity. The nave of Hexham was destroyed by the Scots invaders in 1296, but has been reconstructed in modern times. *Lanercost* (Plate 9) remains one of the most beautiful and characteristic large Augustinian churches in the country, its red stone arches charmingly set amid gigantic sycamores in the valley of the Irthing close to the Roman Wall. The restored nave is still in use as a parish church, but the well-preserved

ruins of the choir, transepts and vaulted refectory undercroft
are preserved by the Ministry of Works.

Of other Augustinian houses *Gisborough Priory*, in the
guardianship of the Ministry, has little left save the eastern gables
of late thirteenth-century date, but at *Kirkham* there remains the
magnificent late thirteenth-century gateway (Plate 5) still
ornamented with fine mediæval sculpture—note especially
St. George and the Dragon, and David and Goliath—as well as a
magnificent series of shields bearing coats of arms of great
importance for the study of early heraldic art. Happily too
the ruined cloister of *Kirkham* retains an enriched lavatory with
traceried panelling of about the year 1300.

The middle of the twelfth century saw the introduction of
those reformations of the Benedictine system designed to secure
greater uniformity of monastic life, more freedom from secular
and episcopal control, and better opportunity to live the religious
life in houses remote from cities, towns and castles. The
earliest of these movements on the Continent was the Cluniac
all of whose priories were dependent on the great Mother Abbey
of Cluny, near Grenoble, which appointed the priors and
controlled the discipline of the daughter houses. As a consequence the Cluniac houses were considered " alien " in
England and were subject to much high-handed spoliation long
before the dissolution. *Monk Bretton* in the midst of the
modern industrial district of Barnsley was founded as a Cluniac
priory by Adam FitzSuain in 1153. The fourteenth-century
gatehouse and the guesthouse remain pratically intact and
there are considerable other remains. The site was handed
over to the Ministry of Works by the Corporation of Barnsley.

Far more important in our area are the remains of later
offshoots of the Benedictine Order. *Furness Abbey* was begun
as a daughter house of the centralized order of Savigny, a
Norman abbey in the diocese of Avranches. But hardly had this
Savignac Order been established in England before it was
absorbed in 1148 in the far greater order of Cîteaux in Burgundy,
founded by St. Stephen Harding, an Englishman, but extended
far and wide through Western Europe by the genius of the most
distinguished son of the Cistercian Order, St. Bernard of
Clairvaux. The strict discipline of the order is embodied in the
" Carta Caritatis," and the rectitude of its early observance made
it popular both with the pious and with lay founders throughout
the North. The first northern Cistercian abbey was *Rievaulx*,

founded in 1131 by Walter L'Espec, Lord of Helmsley. Its first Abbot, William, had been St. Bernard's personal secretary. As early as 1136 *Rievaulx* became the mother house of *Melrose Abbey* in the valley of Tweed, founded by King David I of Scotland. The shrine of St. William the first abbot, who received local if not Roman canonization, was re-discovered in the excavations made by the Ministry of Works immediately to the left of the entrance to the chapter house. *Rievaulx* early became one of the largest and richest Cistercian abbeys in the kingdom, and already in the abbacy of St. Ailred (1147-1167) is said to have housed no less than 140 professed monks and 500 " conversi " or lay brothers. Of twelfth-century work at *Rievaulx* we have only the ruins of the Burgundian nave, transept and great cloister. Its glories, apart from its setting, are the noble thirteenth-century choir (Plate 7) and frater (refectory). These are among the greatest achievements of the so-called Early English style ever built. The immense range of conventual buildings, dormitory, kitchen, infirmary, cloister and hall, tannery, etc., have been once more brought to light by the excavations undertaken by the Ministry of Works.

Only a few miles away another great Cistercian abbey, far more ruined than *Rievaulx*, has also been taken over and ex-cavated by the Ministry of Works, namely, *Byland*, begun on its present site after removal from " old " Byland, in 1177. *Byland* was the largest Cistercian church in England built in accordance with a single design, being 328 feet in total length and 135 feet wide across the transepts. The diameter of the great rose window over the west front, portions of whose tracery have now been unearthed, was 26 feet, one of the largest circular windows in Britain. The whole church and nearly all the buildings belong to the end of the twelfth century. Notable features of *Byland* are the wealth of late twelfth or early thirteenth-century coloured tiles that ornamented the floor, as may now again be seen in one of the transept chapels (Plate 4), and the superb carving of the nave capitals now preserved in the temporary museum on the site.

Another Yorkshire Cistercian abbey in the south of the county, *Roche*, is but a splendid fragment of thirteenth-century design, though the lay-out of the conventual buildings, with their water-courses, is of considerable interest.

At *Furness* (Plate 6) in north-west Lancashire the remains are far more extensive and on a grander scale. The rich red sandstone of which it is built adds colour to the scene.   In addition to the actual buildings there are temporarily housed in the infirmary chapel some of the earliest known freestone effigies of knights in armour in the country.

What St. Bernard accomplished in the way of a reformed and strictly disciplined order for the Benedictine tradition, St. Norbert of Prémontré, near Laon, did for the Augustinian canons regular.   Its chief house in England was Welbeck. The northern abbeys of the Præmonstratensian Order, *Easby*, near Richmond, *Egglestone*, near Barnard Castle, and *Shap* in Westmorland are in the guardianship of the Ministry.   The remains are less spectacular than those of the great Cistercian houses, but *Easby*, founded in 1152, displays the considerable remains of the infirmary on the north side of the church, an irregular trapezoidal cloister, a fine frater on the south side (Plate 10), a western range of most unusual character, and a well-preserved early gate house.

Monasticism in England was at the height of its influence for the two hundred years preceding the Black Death in 1348-49. From this visitation which swept the monasteries they never really recovered.   Thereafter pious benefaction was directed to the endowment of colleges of secular or chantry priests, and to the building or enlargement of parish churches.   Accordingly Perpendicular work is as rare in our monastic remains as it is common in parish or collegiate churches.   Towards the end the monasteries tended to become more and more the life properties of the abbots, who in early Tudor times built for themselves separate and more comfortable accommodation.   But no part of England suffered greater social and economic disturbance than the North from the dissolution of the monasteries under Henry VIII.   That the old foundations still enjoyed widespread affection and support is witnessed by the ill-starred Pilgrimage of Grace.   Apart from the active destruction of monastic buildings at the dissolution, there have been nearly four centuries of neglect.   Only in the last thirty years has this process been arrested, and skill and labour once more employed in the conservation of places that were during turbulent centuries the centres of piety, art, learning and charity.

Two ecclesiastical monuments in the guardianship of the Ministry in the northern counties are more particularly associated with individual anchorites or hermits—namely *Finchale Priory* in Durham and the fourteenth-century Hermitage cut out

of the rock in the valley of the Coquet, near *Warkworth*. The
former, which became an ordinary Benedictine priory of
Durham Cathedral, owes its origin to the solitary piety of
St. Godric, who died early in the twelfth century and whose
oratory was incorporated in the first church; his coffin was
discovered by the Ministry of Works. The rock-cut chapel of
the *Warkworth Hermitage* seems to have been founded about
the year 1350 by a Lord of Warkworth for some individual
recluse, and to have continued with an endowment for a
succession of hermits for several generations. Its romantic
form and situation and the inexplicable sculpured figures in a
niche on the south side of the altar have given rise to numerous
legends, but its exact significance still remains largely a matter
of speculation.

CASTLES

In the six northern counties the Ministry of Works is the
guardian of no fewer than twenty castles or portions of castles
of the mediæval period. These include, both on account of site
and architectural features, some of the finest in the kingdom;
and in no area can the evolution of the English castle be studied
with better examples.

The building of castles was an introduction of the Norman
Conquerors. Before the Conquest practically the only form of
defence was the Anglo-Saxon " burh," consisting of an earthwork with or without a wooden palisade surrounding the
dwellings (also wooden) of a village community. The Norman
castle was essentially different, being the personal military
stronghold of a feudal lord or of the King or of his officer.

During the reigns of William the Conqueror and his
successor Rufus very few castles were constructed in stone,
almost the only certain exceptions being the White Tower of
the *Tower of London*, Colchester, parts of Durham, Tamworth,
and the curtain walls, gatehouse, and hall of *Richmond* in
Yorkshire. The immense number of new Norman castles
made in the eleventh century throughout the country consisted
of an artificial mound or " motte " of earth, surrounded by a
ditch and surmounted by a palisade and other wooden buildings;
attached to it were one or more baileys or courtyards, also
palisaded and surrounded by ditches. The Conqueror's own

twin castles at York on either side of the river were of the motte and bailey type. This original form of Norman castle can be traced at *Pickering* in the vale between York and Scarborough in the North Riding. The motte remains, but its wooden defences were replaced at *Pickering* in the twelfth century by a stone " shell " keep. *Skipsea Castle* in Holderness is an early motte and bailey castle begun soon after the Conquest, though differing from most others of that period in its use of water-defences.

The east and west curtain walls and parts of the gatehouse of the great triangular castle of *Richmond* are among the earliest extant examples of Norman stonework. Characteristic early herring-bone masonry of the Conqueror's reign is still visible. The Honour of Richmond was granted by the King to Alan the Red, son of Eudes, Count of Penthièvre, a near relative of the reigning Duke of Britanny. He held Richmond till 1089 and the main walls were his work. In addition to these walls there remains from this early period in the south-east corner of the inner bailey the eleventh-century stone hall named after Scolland, the sewer of Earl Alan the Red, an almost unique monument of so early a date.

The disastrous reign of Stephen witnessed the growing menace to the State of the building and strengthening of feudal castles by rapacious lordlings, and, in the north, the opportunity for Scottish invasion and destruction, but with the coming of Henry II, one of the most energetic of our mediæval kings, the control of all castles was resumed by the Crown. Many were destroyed, and many were transformed, enlarged and strengthened, either directly by the King or under strict royal licence. During the closing years of Stephen the north had been overrun by the Scots, and it was not until 1157 that Malcolm, King of Scotland, yielded up to Henry II the castles of *Carlisle*, Bamburgh and Newcastle upon Tyne which he had occupied. To the reign and action of Henry II (1154-1189) we owe some of the finest and most remarkable of our great Norman castles, and not least in the northern region.

The great feature of this period was the square keep of ashlar, and of those in State guardianship in the area, *Norham*, *Carlisle*, *Brougham*, *Brough*, *Bowes*, *Helmsley*, *Middleham*, *Richmond*, and *Scarborough* remain witnesses of the immense advance effected in the scale and skill of building craft during the latter half of the twelfth century. The great keep of *Richmond* (Plate

20) built over the earlier gatehouse is over 100 feet high and ranks with Rochester, *Dover*, *Portchester* and Hedingham among the finest twelfth-century towers in the country. *Bowes*, placed in the angle of the old Roman fort and commanding the Yorkshire approach to the Stainmore Pass over the Pennines on the Roman road from York to Carlisle, is unique in that it is the single instance of a great Norman rectangular keep, constructed by Henry II between 1171 and 1187, still unconnected with any other buildings.

More usually the keep was but part of the newly strengthened stone defences of the bailey. In larger castles, which had already one bailey, a new outer bailey, such as the " cockpit " at Richmond, was often added at this period, and the defences of the main entrance to the castle were improved by gate towers and the throwing forward of the gate defences by the erection of a forward building or " barbican."

Apart from " shell " keeps which conformed to the contour of the original motte, rectangular building of subordinate tower defences as well as of the keep was characteristic of most of the twelfth century. Towards the end of this century and in the thirteenth, round and polygonal towers began to take their place. *Conisbrough Castle* (Plate 13), in Yorkshire, which has recently come under the guardianship of the Ministry of Works, has a buttressed circular keep of unusual design, which is one of the finest secular monuments of its age. It was built of fine ashlar, *c.* 1185-90, by Hamelin Plantagenet, and remains practically intact except for the floors and roof, which were of wood. There are some good carved capitals in the chapel, and at the summit the defensive arrangements of a tower of this character may be studied in detail. The curtain which surrounds the courtyard has on it solid round towers, which are amongst the earliest of this kind in the country. The main south gatehouse of *Warkworth* in Northumberland, whose present enceinte was largely the work of Robert FitzRoger in 1199, consists of a pair of polygonal towers (Plate 17) and the angle-turrets of the walls are semi-octagonal. This is among the earliest parts of a castle of quite exceptional interest and magnificence, described by Hamilton Thompson as " the epitome of the history of the castle from its Norman origin to its practical identification in the later Middle Ages with the large Manor house ".

The greater part of the thirteenth century was devoted in the north to the building of abbeys rather than castles, and the new " concentric " type of castle, derived from Syria by the influence of the Crusaders, was not developed here. This new type was adopted by Edward I at *Caernarvon, Conway, Harlech* and *Beaumaris* in his subjugation of the Welsh. It was only in the last years of his reign that this vigorous soldier king turned his attention to his northern frontier, and he died near Carlisle in 1307 on a Scottish campaign. The reign of his weakling successor saw the Scottish victory of Bannockburn, and thereafter the northern counties of England lay under the almost perpetual menace of Scottish raids till the time of Flodden Field. Even later, in the early part of the reign of Elizabeth, *the walls of Berwick-upon-Tweed* were refortified in the " Italian " manner, and it was not until the Union of the Crowns of England and Scotland in 1603 that the North Country could feel any security of peace.

After Bannockburn there was great activity in the building of new castles and the restoration and extension of old. Of castles of this period in the guardianship of the Ministry of Works we may note *Dunstanburgh* on the Northumberland coast, and *Tyne-mouth Castle* guarding the Priory. The fine ruins of *Dunstanburgh* (Plate 19) are the remains of the castle built by Thomas Earl of Lancaster, under a licence granted by Edward II in 1316.

Possessions of the Earldom of Lancaster were not only the castle of Lancaster itself, but, in Yorkshire, Pontefract, Knares-borough and *Pickering*, as well as *Dunstanburgh* in Northumberland. Thomas, Earl of Lancaster, was the cousin of Edward II, being the son of Edmund, younger son of Henry III. As chief of the Lords Ordainers, he was an active opponent of Edward II and his favourites and was the main organizer of the downfall and death of the King's notorious favourite, Piers Gaveston. However, in 1322 he was captured by the King and executed at his own castle of Pontefract. The work at *Dunstanburgh*, especially the great gatehouse keep with its round towers, is mainly his, though additions were made by his more famous successor in the Earldom of Lancaster, John of Gaunt, the son of Edward III.

The most magnificent, best preserved and advanced late mediæval construction is the reconstructed keep of *Warkworth*, probably rebuilt by the first Percy Earl of Northumberland, the father of Harry Hotspur, early in the fifteenth century. The castle of *Penrith* in Cumberland, erected by the Bishops of Carlisle, dates from the fourteenth century, the era when the numerous fortified houses, commonly called Pele Towers, which are widely distributed in the two border counties, were introduced. The fortified gateway to *Steeton Hall* near Pontefract is also of this epoch. That even during the era of stone fortifications important castles continued to rely on protective earthworks is well exemplified by the enormous ditches which form the outer defences of *Helmsley Castle* (Plate 16). In their present form these too seem to date from the fourteenth century, and their excavation by the Ministry of Works reveals the formidable nature of such works.

Of all the castles in the guardianship of the Ministry there are few more splendid than that of *Norham* on the Tweed, a few miles west of Berwick. Norhamshire and Islandshire were two areas geographically in the northern part of the county of Northumberland, but administratively part of the domains of the Bishops Palatine of Durham. The castle of Durham itself and *Norham* were their greatest achievements in military architecture. The scale and magnificence of both are truly remarkable. *Norham*, exposed to the first onslaught of many a Scottish invasion or raid, had need to be strong. Often besieged and damaged, many times repaired and strengthened, its remains show evidence of almost every date between the twelfth and sixteenth centuries inclusive. The greater part of the formidable keep (Plate 14) still standing is the work of Bishop Hugh Puiset towards the end of the twelfth century, and, though in partial ruin, is a fine example of a great Norman fortress. That it successfully withstood sieges even when the Scots had obtained possession of the outer bailey is hardly to be wondered at. The long story of warfare at *Norham* is a terrible revelation of the political consequences of the disunion of the northern and southern kingdoms. What the Wall had been during the Roman occupation, the castles of *Carlisle*, *Norham* and its neighbour, Wark (now almost entirely destroyed) and the fortified town of Berwick-upon-Tweed were throughout the Middle Ages.

NOTES

At a number of monuments for which guide-books are not yet available, the Custodian has a few hand boards on which notes of the history of the building are recorded, together with a plan. These are available for use by the public without charge. Monuments at which official guide-books are on sale are marked with a dagger.

Photographic postcard views of monuments are also on sale, at buildings marked with an asterisk, at 4d. each. Further views are in course of production.

Photographs may be taken by visitors without a permit except at buildings occupied by the military. In these cases the assent of the military must be obtained. The use of stand cameras is subject to the discretion of the Custodian.

Admission Fees. These are indicated under each monument.

Children under fifteen years of age are admitted at half price. At monuments generally, parties of twenty or more visitors are admitted on application to the Custodian at half price. For parties of eleven to twenty in number, the minimum fee is 2s. 6d. or 5s.

Standard Hours of Admission are—

	Weekdays	Sundays
March—April . .	9.30 a.m.—5.30 p.m.	2 p.m.—5.30 p.m.
May—September .	9.30 a.m.—7 p.m.	2 p.m.—7 p.m.
October . . .	9.30 a.m.—5.30 p.m.	2 p.m.—5.30 p.m.
November—February	9.30 a.m.—4 p.m.	2 p.m.—4 p.m.

Variations from the Standard Hours are noted under the particular monument.

CUMBERLAND

†* *Carlisle Castle*

A castle was begun under William Rufus and completed after capture by David, King of the Scots. The keep, probably of the time of Henry II, contains the Regimental Museum of the Border Regiment. Mary, Queen of Scots, occupied a building that stood near the keep.
Situation. Commanding the crossing of the Eden at Carlisle.
Hours of Admission. Standard, but Sundays from 9.30 a.m., May to September.
Admission Fee. 1s.

Castlerigg, the stone circle on (Keswick)

Popularly but wrongly known as Druid's Circle. It consists of 38 standing stones in an oval formation within which at the south-east is an oblong space formed by 10 other stones.
Situation. A mile and a half east of Keswick.
Admission. At any time without charge.

Hardknott Castle, Roman Fort

A fort about 2¾ acres in area, in a commanding position at a height of 800 feet above sea-level, at the head of Eskdale. It was established about A.D. 103. A bath-house and a parade-ground, artificially levelled against the mountainside, lie outside the fort.
Situation. 9 miles north-east of Ravenglass, at the western end of the Hardknott Pass.
Admission. At any time without charge.

* Lanercost Priory (Pl. 9)

Was a house of Augustinian Canons founded about 1144, by William de Vaux. The remains consist of the quire and transepts, the sub-vault of the refectory and parts of the other claustral buildings and of the gatehouse. Tombs of the Dacre and Howard families in the transepts. The nave of the church is still in use as the parish church and is not under the control of the Ministry of Works.
Situation. On the north bank of the Irthing, 2 miles from Brampton, ½ mile south of the Roman Wall.
Hours of Admission. Standard.
Admission Fee. 6d.
A privately-printed guide-book is on sale at this monument.

Penrith Castle

Was built to defend Penrith against Scottish raids. A tower on the site was built by Bishop Strickland of Carlisle. The present courtyard was laid out at the end of the fourteenth century.
Situation. In a public park opposite the railway station.
Admission. Free during hours in which the park is open to the public.

For parts of the Roman Wall, see page 49.

DURHAM

†* Barnard Castle

A castle founded by Guy, lord of Bailleul, and rebuilt by his nephew Bernard Balliol from whom it takes its name. The present remains are mostly of later date, and include parts of a fourteenth-century great hall and a cylindrical keep placed on the precipitous edge of the Durham bank of the River Tees. The castle was besieged in 1569 during the Rising of the Northern Earls.

Situation. In the town of Barnard Castle.
Hours of Admission. Standard.
Admission Fee. 6d.

Bishop Auckland, Auckland Castle Deer House

A deer-shelter in the park of the bishops of Durham. It was built in 1760 by Bishop Trevor and is a good example of the " Gothic " architecture of that time.

Situation. 300 yards north-east of Auckland Castle.
Admission. Without charge, at all hours when the park is open.

†* Finchale Priory

Benedictine priory erected on the site of the chapel of St. Godric (hermit, 1115-70). Considerable remains of the church and claustral buildings dating from the middle of the thirteenth century.

Situation. In a picturesque position on the banks of the River Wear. 5½ miles north of Durham.
Hours of Admission. Standard.
Admission Fee. 1s.

Hylton Castle

A keep-gatehouse built by William de Hylton in the early fifteenth century. Although much altered in the eighteenth and nineteenth centuries, it retains a fine display of mediæval heraldry. A fifteenth and sixteenth-century chapel with half-octagonal transepts stands near the gatehouse.

Situation. 3¾ miles west of Sunderland.
Hours of Admission. Standard.
Admission. Exterior only, without charge.

Jarrow, St. Paul's Monastery

A monastery founded in 682, famous as the home of the Venerable Bede, and refounded as a cell of Durham cathedral-priory in 1075. There are remains of the west and south ranges of the eleventh-century claustral buildings, and the seventh-century monastic church is in use as the chancel of the present parish church.

Situation. Immediately south of Jarrow Parish Church.

LANCASHIRE

†* Furness Abbey and Bow Bridge (Pl. 6)

Was founded in 1127 under the patronage of Stephen, afterwards King of England. The monks were originally of the order of Savigny but later joined the Cistercians. There are extensive remains of the church and monastic buildings. South-east of the ruins, the fifteenth-century Bow Bridge led to one of the abbey mills.

Situation. In the " Glen of Deadly Nightshade " about 1½ miles from Barrow.

Hours of Admission. Standard, but Sundays from 9.30 a.m., May to September.

Admission Fee. 1s.

NORTHUMBERLAND

Berwick-on-Tweed—Castle and Town Walls

The castle was originally built in the twelfth century. All that remains is the west wall with three bastions or towers on its west face. The town walls were originally built by Edward I, but were reconstructed, partly on a new line, under Elizabeth I.

Situation. The castle lies west of the town, by the railway station.

Admission. At any time without charge.

†* *Corbridge (Corstopitum) Roman Station* (Pl. 3)

A Roman site situated at the crossing of the Tyne on the main Roman road from York into Scotland. In the first century an earth and timber fort. In the second and early third centuries, a military base and depot, round which, in the third and fourth centuries, a civil town grew up. Excavated 1907-14, and partly covered up again. The central part of the Roman town has been re-excavated since 1934.

Situation. On north bank of the Tyne between Hexham and Corbridge.

Hours of Admission. Standard, but Sundays from 9.30 a.m., May to September.

Admission Fee. 1s.

†* *Dunstanburgh Castle* (Pl. 19)

The castle stands on high cliffs above the sea and its walls enclose an area of about 9 acres. It was built by Thomas, Earl of Lancaster, in the early fourteenth century and strengthened later by John of Gaunt.

Situation. North of Craster village, about 8 miles north-east of Alnwick.

Access is by a footpath across fields.

Hours of Admission. Standard.

Admission Fee. 6d.

†* *Lindisfarne Priory* (Pl. 12)

The cradle of English Christianity in the north. It was originally an Anglian religious house, founded in A.D. 635 by St. Aidan who came from Iona at the invitation of King Oswald to establish Christianity in his Kingdom. It became the seat of the bishopric of the Northumbrian Kingdom till it was destroyed by the Danes in 875. In 1082 the monastery was re-established as a cell to the Benedictine abbey of Durham.

A large number of interesting stones of the Anglian and Viking periods and a collection of mediæval pottery are preserved in the museum.
Situation. Holy Island.
Hours of Admission. Standard, but Sundays from 9.30 a.m., May to September.
Admission Fee. 1s.

†* *Norham Castle* (Pl. 14)
Was one of the strongest of the border castles and belonged to the Bishops of Durham. Contains the ruins of one of the finest Norman keeps in the country. It was built about 1160 by Bishop Hugh Puiset, and has been much altered at all periods down to the sixteenth century. It was several times besieged by the Scots.
Situation. On the Tweed 8 miles west of Berwick.
Hours of Admission. Standard.
Admission Fee. 1s.

†* *Tynemouth Priory and Castle* (Pl. 11)
There was a monastic foundation here in Anglian times. Destroyed by the Danes 865 and finally abandoned 1008. Refounded in 1090 as a Benedictine priory and a cell of St. Alban's Abbey. The nave dates from this time. The presbytery was rebuilt in the late twelfth and early thirteenth century. Foundations of other monastic building are exposed. A curtain wall with towers and gatehouse-keep was erected in the fourteenth century for defence of the priory. After the dissolution it continued in use by the Crown for coast defence and the walls contain later work.
Situation. Stands on a promontory bounded on the north by Tynemouth Bay and on the south by the River Tyne, 8 miles E. of Newcastle.
Hours of Admission. Standard, but Sundays from 9.30 a.m., May to September.
Admission Fee. 1s.

†* *Warkworth Castle* (Pl. 17)
The earlier remains date from the twelfth century and it was much altered in the thirteenth. In the fourteenth century it came into the possession of the Percys, Earls of Northumberland, who built the magnificent keep in the early fifteenth century. It is still the property of the Duke of Northumberland.
Situation. On River Coquet 7½ miles south-east of Alnwick.
Hours of Admission. Standard, but Sundays from 9.30 a.m., May to September.
Admission Fee. 1s.

†* *Warkworth Hermitage*
An interesting Hermitage consisting of a small chapel cut in solid rock with living-rooms adjoining. It dates from the fourteenth century. Access is by rowing boat from the castle.
Situation. About ½ mile from the castle up the River Coquet.
Hours of Admission. Standard, but closed in winter.
Admission Fee. 1s. (includes passage by boat).

For parts of the Roman Wall see pages 46-8.

WESTMORLAND

Arthur's Round Table, Penrith

A prehistoric earthwork consisting of roughly circular area 150 feet by 160 feet in diameter bounded by a ditch with a bank on the outside.
Situation. Immediately west of the main road at Eamont Bridge, 1 mile south of Penrith.
Admission. At any time without charge.

†* *Brough Castle*

Considerable remains of keep of about 1170 standing in a prominent position on a hill with other buildings of later periods surrounding a paved courtyard.
It was burnt down by the Scots in 1521 and repaired in the middle of the seventeenth century by Anne Countess of Pembroke.
Situation. Within the Roman Fort of Verterae, 8 miles south-east of Appleby just off the main road to Barnard Castle.
Hours of Admission. Standard.
Admission Fee. 6d.

†* *Brougham Castle* (Pl. 15)

There are extensive remains of the keep of about 1170 and of other buildings of later periods.
It was finally added to and repaired by the Countess of Pembroke in the middle of the seventeenth century.
Situation. On the site of the Roman Fort of Brocavum on the south bank of the River Eamont just below its confluence with the River Lowther 1½ miles east of Penrith.
Hours of Admission. Standard.
Admission Fee. 6d.

Mayborough, near Penrith

An oval area surrounded by a bank of stones and earth. There is no ditch ; near the centre is a large stone.
Situation. West of Eamont Bridge, 1 mile south of Penrith.
Admission. At any time without charge.

Shap Abbey

A Præmonstratensian abbey founded *c.* 1180 at Preston Patrick and moved to Shap *c.* 1199. Most of the buildings are of thirteenth-century date, but the main feature is the early sixteenth-century west tower.
Situation. A mile west of Shap village.
Hours of Admission. Standard.
Admission Fee. 6d.

YORKSHIRE

Aldborough (Isurium Brigantum) Roman Town

The capital of the Brigantes, the largest tribe in Roman Britain. Part of the south-west angle of the Roman town wall and two mosaic pavements within the town are in the charge of the Ministry. There is a museum of objects found in former excavations.
Situation. In Aldborough village, ¾ mile east of Boroughbridge.
Admission Fee. To the museum and town wall, 6*d*.

* *Bowes Castle*

A massive stone keep three storeys high dating from *c.* 1170.
Situation. Within the Roman Fort of Lavatrae on the main road 4 miles west of Barnard Castle just west of the church.
Hours of Admission. Standard.
Admission. Free.

†* *Burton Agnes Norman Manor House*

Good example of a Norman house, such as is common in the south of England, but rare in the north. It was encased in brick when the adjacent Hall was built early in the seventeenth century.
Situation. In the village.
Hours of Admission. At any time without charge.

†* *Byland Abbey* (Pl. 4)

A colony from the Savignac abbey of Furness, after some vicissitudes, having joined the Cistercian Order, settled at Byland in 1177. The considerable remains of the church and monastic buildings date from the late twelfth and early thirteenth centuries. The glazed tiles which cover a large part of the floor of the nave and transepts are particularly well preserved.
Situation. A mile north-east of the village of Coxwold, between Thirsk and Helmsley.
Hours of Admission. Standard.
Admission Fee. 1*s*.

†* *Conisbrough Castle*

Circular keep built *c.* 1185-90 by Hamelin Plantagenet remains almost to its full height. Curtain of little later date has unusual solid round towers.
Situation. 4½ miles south-west of Doncaster.
Hours of Admission. Standard, but Sundays from 9.30 a.m., May to September.
Admission Fee. 1*s*.

†* *Easby Abbey* (Pl. 10)

A Præmonstratensian abbey dedicated to St. Agatha, founded 1155. The church has mostly disappeared, but there are very considerable remains of the monastic buildings of most unusual plan dating from the early thirteenth century. The frater, remodelled about 1300, is particularly fine.
Situation. On the banks of the River Swale, in a delightful setting about a mile east of Richmond.
Hours of Admission. Standard.
Admission Fee. 6d.

†* *Egglestone Abbey*

Picturesque remains of a Præmonstratensian abbey. The greater part of the nave (twelfth to fourteenth century) and the chancel (thirteenth century) are still standing, with remains of the claustral buildings.
Situation. On the right bank of the River Tees about 1½ miles south of Barnard Castle.
Hours of Admission. Standard.
Admission Fee. 6d.

†* *Gisborough Priory*

A priory of Augustinian Canons founded in the first half of the twelfth century. Fine remains of east end of church of early fourteenth-century date and a twelfth-century gatehouse are all that remain above ground. The earlier church was burnt down in 1289.
Situation. Immediately to the south of the parish church.
Hours of Admission. Standard.
Admission Fee. 6d.

†* *Helmsley Castle* (Pl. 16)

The keep and curtain wall and towers were begun at the end of the twelfth century by Robert de Roos. In the middle of the sixteenth century a block of domestic buildings was constructed against the western curtain wall. Besieged during the Civil War.
The earthworks surrounding the castle are exceptionally fine.
Situation. In the town of Helmsley, 12 miles east of Thirsk.
Hours of Admission. Standard, but Sundays from 9.30 a.m., May to September.
Admission Fee. 1s.

†* *Kirkham Priory* (Pl. 5)

A house of Augustinian Canons founded by Walter L'Espec about 1125. The remains are extensive with a fine lavatorium and a gatehouse which has a remarkable display of late thirteenth-century heraldry.
Situation. On the bank of the Derwent. About 12 miles north-east of York. 5 miles south-west of New Malton.
Hours of Admission. Standard, but Sundays from 9.30 a.m., May to September.
Admission Fee. 6d.

†* *Middleham Castle*

Begun about 1170 by Robert Fitz Randolph. The fine keep of this date stands in the centre of an inner ward of thirteenth-century date with later additions.
Situation. In Wensleydale, 2 miles south of Leyburn.
Hours of Admission. Standard.
Admission Fee. 6d.

†* *Monk Bretton Priory*

An important Cluniac house, with considerable remains of the church and claustral buildings. Part of the western range was much altered for a residence in the late seventeenth century. The fine gatehouse is incorporated in farm buildings.
Situation. About 2 miles north-east of Barnsley just off the main road to Pontefract.
Hours of Admission. Standard.
Admission Fee. 6d.

†* *Mount Grace Priory*

The finest example of a charterhouse or Carthusian monastery in the country. It was founded in 1398 by Thomas Holland, Duke of Surrey, and the existing remains include the outer court with its gatehouse, guesthouses and barns, the great cloister with the cells of the monks, and the monastic church. The Priory was placed in the guardianship of the Ministry by the National Trust.
Situation. 7 miles north-east of Northallerton.
Hours of Admission. May to September, 9 a.m. to 7 p.m.; October to February, 9.30 a.m. to 4 p.m.; March and April, 9 a.m. to 6 p.m. Sundays from 2 p.m. *Closed Mondays.*
Admission Fee. 1s.

†* *Pickering Castle*

Considerable remains of late eleventh or early twelfth-century castle with a shell keep standing on a fine motte. Curtain walls and towers mostly date from the fourteenth century.
Situation. On the north side of the town.
Hours of Admission. Standard.
Admission Fee. 1s.

†* *Richmond Castle* (Pl. 20)

Richmond Castle occupies a strong position commanding Swaledale. It was first built in the eleventh century, and remains of the gatehouse, hall and curtain wall of that date exist. The keep, one of the finest in the country, is of the twelfth century. By the middle of the sixteenth century the castle had fallen into disrepair.
Situation. Standing above River Swale, overlooking town of Richmond.
Hours of Admission. Standard, but Sundays from 9.30 a.m., May to September.
Admission Fee. 1s.

Plate 13.   CONISBROUGH CASTLE.   THE KEEP.

Plate 14.   NORHAM CASTLE.   THE KEEP,

Plate 15. BROUGHAM CASTLE. GATEHOUSE AND KEEP.

Plate 16.   HELMSLEY CASTLE FROM THE WEST.

Plate 17. WARKWORTH CASTLE. THE KEEP.

Plate 18. SCARBOROUGH CASTLE. THE KEEP.

Plate 19. DUNSTANBURGH CASTLE. GATEHOUSE-KEEP.

Plate 20. RICHMOND CASTLE. THE KEEP.

†* Rievaulx Abbey (Pl. 7)

The abbey was begun by the Cistercian monks about A.D. 1132. The nave is the earliest large Cistercian nave in Britain and it is older than any now standing in France. It dates from about A.D. 1135-1140. The choir is one of the finest examples of the work of the thirteenth century. The extensive monastic buildings are well preserved.

Situation. Beautifully situated in Ryedale, 3 miles north-east of Helmsley.
Hours of Admission. Standard, but Sundays from 9.30 a.m., May to September.
Admission Fee. 1s.

†* Roche Abbey

Cistercian abbey founded in 1147. Of the church only the walls of the north and south transepts are still standing to their full height, but the remains of the whole of the monastic buildings are extensive. A fine gatehouse lies to the north-west of the church.

Situation. In a picturesque valley 1½ miles south of Maltby, 8 miles west of Rotherham.
Hours of Admission. Standard.
Admission Fee. 6d.

Salley Abbey

A Cistercian abbey founded in 1148 by William de Percy. A fairly complete ground-plan of the building remains, and the abbey church is of particular interest in that, although originally designed on a large scale, the poverty of the house resulted in the building of an aisleless nave only 40 feet long.

Situation. Close to the main road, 3 miles south-west of Gisburn and 1¾ miles north-east of Chatburn.
Admission. At any time without charge.

†* Scarborough Castle (Pl. 18)

Remains of twelfth-century castle with keep which dominates the town of Scarborough. Besieged twice and taken by the Parliamentarians 1645 and 1648. It was also damaged by shell fire during the 1914-1918 War. George Fox, the Quaker, was imprisoned here in 1665. On the edge of the cliff are the remains of the fourth-century Roman Signal Station.

Situation. On the high cliff overlooking the sea to the east of the town.
Hours of Admission. Standard, but Sundays from 9.30 a.m., May to September.
Admission Fee. 1s.

Skipsea Castle

A large circular Norman motte separated from the bailey by a level space formerly covered with water, known as Skipsea Mere. A causeway led across the Mere to the bailey, which was of large size, covering 8½ acres. Only the outer bailey is in the charge of the Ministry of Works.

Situation.   9 miles south of Bridlington, 5 miles north of Hornsea.
Admission.   At any time without charge.

* Spofforth Castle

An early fourteenth-century building with interesting detail. There are the remains of a hall and a solar wing on the first floor. One wall of the ground floor is formed by the living rock.

Situation.   5 miles south-east of Harrogate.
Hours of Admission: Standard.
Admission Fee.   6d.

Stanwick Fortifications

Earthwork fortifications of great extent, enclosing an area of 850 acres, probably erected by King Venutius as a rallying point for the Brigantes at the time of the Roman conquest of Yorkshire. An excavated section of the rampart and rock-cut ditch are in the charge of the Ministry.

Situation.   Between Stanwick and Forcett churches, 10 miles west of Darlington.
Admission.   At any time without charge.

Steeton Hall Gateway

A late fourteenth-century gatehouse with interesting heraldic decoration.
Situation.   8 miles west of Selby.
Admission.   Without charge ; key for the interior kept by R. Sunderland & Sons, Ltd., Saw Mill, South Milford.

Wheeldale Moor, Roman Road (Pl. 2)

A stretch of the Roman road leading north from the camps at Cawthorn across Wheeldale Moor. Probably dates from the end of the first century. The section under the guardianship of the Ministry of Works is more than a mile in length and runs from Wheeldale Bridge towards Goathland.

Situation.   2 miles south of Goathland Station, west of the Pickering-Whitby road.
Admission.   At any time without charge.

†* *Whitby Abbey* (Pl. 8)

Site of early Saxon monastery founded in 657 with St. Hilda, a Northumbrian princess, as abbess. Destroyed by the Danes about 870, but reoccupied and refounded as a Benedictine abbey towards the end of the eleventh century. There are considerable remains of the fine church dating from the thirteenth century. Damaged by shell fire during the 1914-1918 War.

Situation. Standing above the town of Whitby on a hill to the east.
Hours of Admission. Standard, but Sundays from 9.30 a.m., May to September.
Admission Fee. 1s.

†* *Clifford's Tower, York Castle*

This tower was erected in the mid-thirteenth century. It stands on one of two mottes thrown up by William the Conqueror to hold York 1068-69. There are some remains of the curtain wall and towers of the bailey.

Situation. In the southern part of the city of York.
Hours of Admission. Standard, but Sundays from 9.30 a.m., May to September.
Admission Fee. 6d.

ROMAN WALL

The Wall was built by the Emperor Hadrian *c.* A.D. 121-126 to control the frontier of the Empire. It runs from Wallsend to Bowness-on-Solway, 73½ miles. At every Roman mile there was a " milecastle " and between each pair of milecastles two turrets. At its eastern end the Wall was always of stone, and from Newcastle for some twenty miles westward was 9 feet thick ; but from there to the River Irthing, though the foundation is for the most part " broad " the superstructure is " narrow "—7 ft. 9 in. thick. West of the Irthing the Wall was originally built of turf or clay, as were the outer walls of the milecastles, which had internal buildings of wood ; the turrets, however, were of stone ; this western section of the wall was gradually rebuilt from east to west in stone 7 ft. 6 in. thick. The Wall from Newcastle to Wallsend, which is of the same thickness, is also a later feature.

The numbers given to the sections of the Wall are based on the now generally accepted numeration of the milecastles and turrets westwards from Wallsend. The first turret west of each milecastle is lettered ' a ', the second ' b '.

South of the Wall ran a communication-road known as the Military Way and south of that again, at varying distances from the Wall, the imposing earthwork now called the Vallum and consisting of a wide flat-bottomed ditch flanked by mounds composed of the upcast.
Admission. At any time without charge unless otherwise stated.

NORTHUMBERLAND

(1) *Benwell* (*Condercum*)

An original causeway across the Vallum ditch to give access to Condercum fort, which lay to the north.
Situation. At the bottom of Denhill Park.

(2) *Benwell Roman Temple*

A small temple with the apse at the south end. Two altars dedicated to the gods Anociticus and Antenociticus were found here in 1862 and casts of them are on the site, the originals being in the Blackgate Museum, Newcastle.
Situation. In Broomridge Avenue.

(3) *Denton Hall Turret* (No. 7b)

A section of Wall 70 yards long and a turret which retains the base of the platform on which rested a ladder giving access to the upper floor.
Situation. On the south side of the main road from Newcastle, west of Denton Burn.

(4) *West Denton*

A stretch of 70 yards of Wall which, though much reduced, shows some of the very large stones characteristic of the east end of the Wall.
Situation. About 250 yards west of the preceding.

(5) *Heddon-on-the-Wall*

A fine stretch of 280 yards of the Wall with clearly marked ditch. The circular chamber near its west end is a mediæval kiln.
Situation. On the south side of the Newcastle road, north-east of Heddon-on-the-Wall village.

(6) *Section near Planetrees Farm* (No. 26). A length of 50 feet of narrow

wall on broad foundation showing extensive rebuilding in Roman times.
Situation. On the south side of the Newcastle-Carlisle road one mile east of Chollerford.

(7) *Brunton Turret* (No. 26b). One of the best preserved on the line of

the Wall ; and a 70 yard stretch of Wall.
Situation. ½ mile east of Chollerford ; access by a stile on the Hexham road, 350 yards south of the crossroads.

†*(8) *Chesters* (*Cilurnum*) *Roman Fort Baths and Bridge Abutment.*

The Wall from the railway to the river (about 150 yards) is in the Ministry's care, but has not been uncovered, except at its west end where it is seen to be rebuilt where it joins the abutment at a square tower. The massive splayed abutment suggests that the bridge carried a road about 20 feet wide. There were four arches and traces of two of the water-piers and of the west abutment can be seen when the river is low. Evidence of an earlier, narrower bridge is seen in a hexagonal mass of masonry incorporated in the eastern abutment. Crossing the line of the abutment and the turret is a large covered drain which was probably the mill-race of a water-mill.

The fort, occupying nearly six acres and designed for a garrison of five hundred cavalry, lies on rising ground west of the site of the bridge. The gateways, headquarters buildings, commandant's house, and barracks are exposed. Between the fort and the bridge are the extensive ruins of the bath house.

North of the fort, the Clayton Memorial Museum contains a magnificent collection of Roman inscriptions, sculptures and other objects.

Situation. The Bridge Abutment is ½ mile south-west of Chollerford on the left bank of the North Tyne. *Access* by a pathway along the west side of the railway line.

The Fort, Baths, and Museum are on the right bank. *Access* from the Chollerford-Walwick road.

Admission Fee. To the Fort, Baths and Museum, 1*s.*
Hours of Admission :

	Weekdays	*Sundays*
March—April .	. 9 a.m. to 5 p.m.	2 p.m. to 4.30 p.m.
May—September	. 9 a.m. to 5.30 p.m.	2 p.m. to 5 p.m.
October—February .	9.30 a.m. to 4 p.m.	2 p.m. to 4 p.m.

A privately printed guide-book is on sale at this monument.

(9) *Carrawburgh, Temple of Mithras.*

A *mithraeum* built outside the fort at Carrawburgh (Procolitia) early in the third century, and remodelled four times before its desecration, probably in A.D. 324.

Situation. 4 miles north-west of Chollerford on the Greenhead road.

(10) Section at *Sewingshields,* including milecastles Nos. 34 and 35 and turrets Nos. 33b-35b.

Two Roman miles of the Wall are here in the Ministry's care, but the Wall itself was largely removed by stone-robbers in the early nineteenth century, though there are traces of the milecastles and turrets. The most interesting portion is the eastern 700 yards next to the road. Here, though the Wall is gone, both Vallum and Military Way are very well preserved, as is the Wall ditch which dies away beyond the mile-castle where the rise of the crags makes it unnecessary.

Situation. North of the Newcastle-Carlisle road, 7 miles west of Chollerford and 4 miles east of the " Twice Brewed " Inn.

†*(11) *Housesteads (Borcovicium) Roman Fort*

A five-acre fort for a garrison of a thousand infantry. The walls, turrets, gateways, headquarters building and granaries can be seen.

South of the fort there was an extensive *vicus* or civil settlement. A museum on the site contains altars, inscriptions and models. The fort was placed in the guardianship of the Ministry by the National Trust. *Situation.* 2¾ miles north-east of Bardon Mill and ½ mile north of the Newcastle-Carlisle road.

Hours of Admission. Standard, but Sundays from 9.30 a.m., May to September.
Admission Fee. 1s.

(12) *Chesterholm (Vindolanda) Roman Fort and milestone*

This 3½ acre fort lies 2 miles south of the Wall but belongs to the main defensive system, though not part of the original Wall scheme. The earliest occupation dates from the time of Agricola whose road, the Stanegate, runs past the north gate of the fort and retains, near the burn, a Roman milestone ; the base of another (not in the Ministry's guardianship) stands a Roman mile to the west. Though there is evidence of late second-century and third-century structures, the fort in its present form is of early fourth-century date, with alterations of *c.* 370. The main exposed feature is the notable early fourth-century headquarters building.

Situation. 1 mile north of Bardon Mill Station, and 1 mile south-east of the ' Twice Brewed ' Inn on the Newcastle-Carlisle road.

(13) *Winshields Milecastle* (No. 40)

A fine stretch of 350 yards of Wall, including at its eastern end Winshields Milecastle. This stretch includes the highest point on the Wall, 1,230 feet above sea-level. The thickness of the Wall here, as elsewhere on the steep crags, is 7 ft. 6 ins.

Situation. On the summit of the crags to the north of the 'Twice Brewed' Inn. Access by footpath from the road leading north from the Inn.

(14) *Cawfields Milecastle* (No. 42)

A stretch of almost ¾ mile of Wall running along the top of Cawfield Crags from the well-preserved milecastle No. 42 on the west to the Caw Gap on the east.

Situation. ¼ mile north of the Newcastle-Carlisle road between Shield-on-the-Wall and the Haltwhistle Burn.

(15) *Section on Walltown Crags* (No. 45a)

Turret 45a is unusual as being 100 yards short of the normal turret position and as having been built before the Wall of which 400 yards are here in the Ministry's care. It is possible that, because of its commanding position, this turret was part of some long-distance signalling system.

Situation. ½ mile north of Newcastle-Carlisle road—½ mile east of Greenhead.

CUMBERLAND

(16) *Poltross Burn Milecastle*

Poltross Burn milecastle (No. 48) excavated 1909. Junction of its broad west wing-wall with narrow wall on broad foundation exposed in edge of railway embankment.
Access by footpath from Gilsland railway station south of line.

(17) *Gilsland (Vicarage garden)*

220 yards of Wall west of railway line showing narrow Wall on broad foundation in the Vicarage garden.
Access from Gilsland—Low Row road between Vicarage and School.

(18) *Willowford Bridge Abutment*

1,000 yards of Wall, including turrets 48a and b, running west from the Low Row road and ending at Willowford bridge abutment. The latter, with about 30 yards of the adjacent Wall, which has been excavated and retains the wing-wall and north-east corner of an original turret and a later tower, was much altered in Roman times owing to changes in the course of the River Irthing and the introduction of a water-mill.
Access from Low Row road near Roman Wall Villa.

(19) *Harrow's Scar Milecastle* (No. 49)

Harrow's Scar milecastle, on the west of the Irthing, marks the beginning of the Turf Wall. The Stone Wall, which here replaced it on a slightly different line, is in the Ministry's charge as far as a point about 500 yards west of Birdoswald.

(20) *Birdoswald (Camboglanna)*

This five-acre fort was designed to hold a thousand infantry and had four main gateways and two posterns ; the east gateway and recently excavated fort walls are particularly well preserved. The interior of the fort is in private ownership.
Admission to Birdoswald fort must be sought at farmhouse.

(21) *Piper Sike Turret* (No. 51a)

A " Turf Wall " turret, built before the Stone Wall, which abuts against the turret's east and west walls.
Situation. About 2½ miles north-east of Lanercost Priory.

(22) *Leahill Turret* (No. 51b)

A " Turf Wall " turret similar to (21). The narrow berm or flat space between the turret and the ditch is typical of " Turf Wall " structures.
Situation. About 540 yards west of (21).

(23) *Banks East Turret* (No. 52)

Another " Turf Wall " turret, in a good state of preservation. The plinth at the front and back is characteristic of " Turf Wall " turrets.
Situation. 4 miles west of Gilsland and 1½ miles N.E. of Lanercost Priory.

BIBLIOGRAPHY

Generally

ROYAL COMMISSION ON HISTORICAL MONUMENTS (England). Inventory for Westmorland.
THE NORTHUMBERLAND COUNTY HISTORY.
THE VICTORIA COUNTY HISTORIES.
KENDRICK, T. D., AND HAWKES, C. F. C. Archæology in England and Wales, 1914-1931.
THE OXFORD HISTORY OF ENGLAND.

Prehistoric Period

ALLCROFT, G. H. Earthworks of England, 1908.
ELGEE, F. The Archæology of Yorkshire, 1933.
ORDNANCE SURVEY. Field Archæology, 1932.
CLARK, J. G. D. Prehistoric England, 1948.
PIGGOTT, S. British Prehistory, 1949.

Roman Period

BRUCE, J. C. Handbook to the Roman Wall. (Revised 1957).
RICHMOND, I. A. Roman Britain, 1955.
HAVERFIELD, F. J. Roman Occupation of Britain, 1924.
    ,,   Romanization of Roman Britain (Revised 1923).
ORDNANCE SURVEY. Map of Roman Britain, 3rd Edition, 1956.
QUENNELL, M. and C. Everyday Life in Roman Britain, 1924.

ORDNANCE SURVEY. Map of Britain in the Dark Ages, 1938.

Ecclesiastical Buildings

THOMPSON, A. H. English Monasteries, 1923.
THOMPSON, A. H. The Ground Plan of the English Parish Church.
POWER, E. E. Mediæval English Nunneries, 1922.
CLAPHAM, A. W. English Romanesque Architecture after the Conquest, 1934.
GRAHAM, ROSE. An Essay on English Monasteries (Historical Association Pamphlet No. 112), 1939.
GILYARD-BEER, R. Abbeys, 1958.
ORDNANCE SURVEY. Map of Monastic Britain.

Castles

THOMPSON, A. H. Military Architecture in England during the Middle Ages, 1912.
ARMITAGE, E. S. Early Norman Castles, 1912.
O'NEIL, B. H. ST. J. Castles, 1953.
BROWN, R. ALLEN. English Medieval Castles, 1954.

INDEX

S.O. Code No. 67-9-1-59